T0018845

The Little Book of

First published in Great Britain in 2023 by Greenfinch
An imprint of Quercus Editions Ltd
Carmelite House
50 Victoria Embankment
London
EC4Y 0DZ

An Hachette UK company

A CIP catalogue record for this book is available from the British Library.

HB ISBN 978-1-52943-714-0
eBook ISBN 978-1-52943-715-7

10 9 8 7 6 5 4 3 2 1

Commissioned by Emily Arbis
Text by Christy White-Spunner
Design by Ginny Zeal

Printed and bound in the United States of America

The Little Book of

Kenergy

UNOFFICIAL AND UNAUTHORIZED

greenfinch

An Introduction to Kenergy

Mother Teresa once said, "A life not lived for others is not a life." We now understand that she was referring to Kenergy. And if we dig into her language, she's basically saying anyone who doesn't have Kenergy needs to get "a life."

This new phenomenon is capturing hearts, redefining masculinity, and doubling sunglasses sales across the world. But what is Kenergy? More importantly, how do you achieve it?

Put simply, Kenergy is main-sidekick-character energy. It's the noble act of playing second fiddle, devoting your life to making someone else look good, supporting from the sidelines like it's the main stage. And looking fresh as hell while you're at it.

Yes, as Mother Teresa insinuated, it's what's on the outside that counts. Strong Kenergy means taking great care over your appearance, not out of vanity, but to make your girlfriend pop even harder. You should be her most stylish accessory, by her side whenever she requires, in coordinating colors, with a perma-tan, muscles so strong each one is named after a feminist icon, and a smile so sparkling that people ask if you've had your teeth vajazzled.

The more you focus on your exterior, the less you have to worry about your interior. Having thoughts takes up precious space in your brain that could be used for anticipating your girlfriend's every want and need, not to mention frantically hoping she notices you. Crucially though, you do need to seem to have an interesting inside—or, to use a technical term, "personality"—to get her attention. Fortunately, a few choice moves or accessories—books, an earring, a perfected "thinking pose"—can give you the illusion of depth without any of the distracting, unwanted thoughts that come with it.

Don't keep a lid on your feelings though. Real Kenergy is about wearing your heart on your forearm (avoid long sleeves; they hide your muscles). Emotions are great for making her fall in love with you, so long as those emotions are love, humility, gratitude, and loyalty. (Anything more unsavory is best expelled covertly via aggressive hot dancing). Plus, following your heart and sense of wonder can take you to cool places, like the zoo, which not only make you seem cute but also give you a tiny unpredictable edge, which she'll find hard to resist.

Ultimately, Kenergy is about making the woman you love feel special, and being so humble and talented at it that she won't even question it. Stay two steps ahead at seeming like you're one step behind her. If this is confusing, don't worry. Read on to find a bank of Kenergy examples that will help you wrestle this kind, elusive beast into something coherent and actionable. Keep your trusty Kenergy book on you at all times, and soon you'll be overflowing with the stuff. It won't be long before you're ready to serve the woman you love, win her heart, and at the very least share a moment with her. That's the real reward.

Examples of Kenergy

Hides in his girlfriend's suitcase to surprise her on vacation, then happily gets the six-hour flight home alone when she doesn't want him there.

Waits patiently for crippling intrusive thoughts to pass, then merrily resumes making a round of strawberry daiquiris.

Constantly tinkering with his top five karaoke choices. They're all by Dua Lipa.

Sleeps in an eye mask with his girlfriend's eyes printed on it so she can see something beautiful when she wakes up.

Refuses to
acknowledge
erections that
aren't caused by
his girlfriend.

Polishes his motorcycle every morning just in case he learns to ride it one day.

Once had
to be rescued by
a lifeguard after
following a family
of turtles out
to sea.

Proudly displays an empty Microaggression Jar in his apartment.

Anonymously leaves positive motivational messages as his coworkers' screensavers after everyone's gone home.

Quickly runs home to change when he realizes his outfit doesn't go with his date's. Then returns, smiles, and says, "Sorry, now I can focus."

Lets his girlfriend test out her makeup ideas on him first to check they look good.

Texts the boys to meet up an hour before a party so they can practice their group dance routine. If anyone says no, he replies, "No worries. I know you'll crush it anyway :)"

Writes LinkedIn endorsements for all of his friends, praising their "inner beauty and poise" in industries he doesn't understand.

Had to ban himself from the pound because he was rescuing too many dogs.

Sneaks off to another room to secretly fist pump the air when someone compliments his appearance.

Challenges the bouncer to a dance-off to secure free entry into the club.

Writes *Black Beauty* fan fiction, but it's just pictures of horses.

Tries to lead his subway car in a group breathing session to kickstart an awesome day.

Posts a black-and-white selfie of him looking hot at a war memorial, with the caption, "*Literally so sad.*"

Carries a chic CamelBak to make sure everyone stays hydrated. He fills it with rosé for special occasions.

Starts a conga
line at parties
and doesn't finish
them until the last
person is safely
dropped off at
their door at the
end of the night.

Cries when contestants have their food criticized on cooking shows.

Keeps leaving hints around the house that he wants his girlfriend to propose.

Organizes pillow fights for anyone who's been looking a little down recently.

If you give him
a mile, he takes
an inch.

Tracks his girlfriend's menstrual cycle so he can stay one step ahead of her needs.

Pauses the song whenever a female rapper says, "I slept with your man," to assure his girlfriend it's not true.

Only ever interrupts his girlfriend to suggest being kinder to herself.

Can't buy his girlfriend a purse, jewelry, or piece of clothing without buying himself a "his" version.

Makes his girlfriend a packed lunch every day, with handwritten poems hidden inside the sandwiches.

Gently lays a blanket over anyone who falls asleep on the subway.

Being kicked off
the cheerleading
team in college for
being too positive.

Performs slam poetry based on things his girlfriend says while she's asleep.

Ensures he's up to date on all the TV shows his girlfriend's watching in case she needs to discuss them.

Regularly gives himself pep talks in the mirror, saying, "You go out there and show her how much she means to you!"

Completed a
BA degree
in photography
to help him be a
better Instagram
boyfriend.

Every year,
he observes a
minute's silence
to commemorate
Madonna falling
off the stage at
the Brits.

If the restaurant bill is put in front of him instead of his girlfriend, he raises an eyebrow at the waiter and slowly slides it into the middle of the table.

Refuses to listen to Britney in protest of her conservatorship. And it's killing him.

Names his biceps
Greta and Malala.

Knows where the nearest pool is at any time so he can jump into it if he's about to cry.

Does three outfit changes over the course of an evening in.

Writes down ideas for nail polish names in his spare time.

Kills houseplants by being too attentive.

Tried to get the songs in his Spotify Wrapped to spell out his girlfriend's name but messed it up because he couldn't stop listening to Billie Eilish.

Gets mugged constantly.

Always covertly texts his girlfriend's friends before a party to make sure none of them are wearing the same thing.

Always yells,
"Is this OK?!" as
he comes.

Saves mosquitos, nurses them back to health, but finds it too emotional to set them free again.

Aggressively dances trauma away.

Within a few minutes, he'll have the entire bus singing, "Man! I Feel Like a Woman!"

Does a little celebration dance when the pizza arrives.

Makes snacks and cocktails for girls' night then role-plays as their French waiter, Raphael, never breaking character.

Calls people he's only known for a few days and says, "Okay, stop what you're doing and look how beautiful the moon is right now."

His favorite part of boys' night is the walk home in the twilight listening to Phoebe Bridgers.

Wears a bra,
partly to support
his enormous pecs,
but mostly out
of solidarity.
Regularly burns it.

Names his
firstborn son
after his wife.

Refuses to name his penis but calls his butt Shakira.

Can't stop blowing all his money at the same bar cause the bartender calls him "my guy."

Spends hours arranging his child's soft animals so they've all got someone to talk to.

Sets alarms for the middle of the night so he can gaze at his girlfriend sleeping (but often wakes her up by accidentally saying "wow" out loud).

Likes to say, "The perfect woman doesn't exist . . ." whenever he's walking into a room his girlfriend's in, then stops in his tracks and slowly takes off his sunglasses.

Sets daily phone reminders to check his privilege.

Hires an events team for Valentine's Day.

Insists on taking
his wife's name
in marriage.

Sets his girlfriend's daily horoscope as his homepage.

Has a loud fart ready at all times in case his girlfriend does something embarrassing and he needs to divert attention away from her.

Saves his girlfriend's leftover crusts, popsicle sticks, and nail clippings for his shrine.

Spends hours
rehearsing what
he's going to
say during sex
that night, then
apologizes
profusely when he
gets his lines
wrong.

Once missed a job interview because he sprinted off to find the end of a rainbow.

Describes every ex as the one that got away, but his girlfriend as the love of his life.

Always wanted
to be Robin
when playing
superheroes as
a kid.

Gets carried away chasing butterflies and ends up miles away from home.

Writes original chants to sing at his children's sports games, specifying that whatever happens he still loves them.

Plays as Luigi in Mario Kart.

Hires a stylist for when he first meets his girlfriend's parents.

Tries to Shazam his girlfriend's farts.

Brings a framed picture of his girlfriend to the gym for inspiration.

Occasionally treats himself by adopting an elephant on his own behalf.

Cries happy tears when his girlfriend gives him hug coupons for his birthday.

Can magic
a romantic
picnic from
thin air, anytime,
anywhere, in four
different styles of
cuisine.

Toasts, "To the women who paved the way" whenever he takes a first sip of any drink.

Says things to passers-by like, "We are not worthy of that outfit."

Refuses to use any dating app except Bumble.

Always secretly
wears a pair of
rip-off trousers
in case he needs
to cause a
distraction.

Records his own audiobook of whatever book his girlfriend's reading in case she wants to listen while driving.

Says, "Thank you, I needed that today" whenever a dog looks at him.

Spends all day writing and rehearsing a one-man play for his girlfriend when she gets home from work but then gets stage fright and can't perform.

Likes wearing nothing but his girlfriend's shirt around the apartment after making love.

Regularly tells his gerbil that it's the only person who understands him.